George Washington:
Hero of the American Revolution

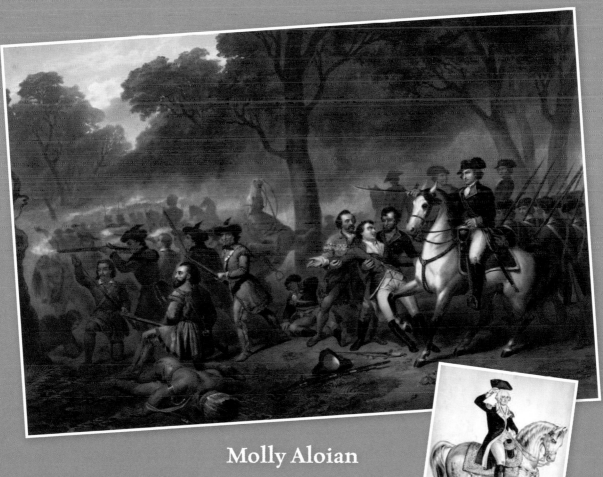

Molly Aloian

CRABTREE
Publishing Company
www.crabtreebooks.com

Author: Molly Aloian

Publishing plan research and development:
Sean Charlebois, Reagan Miller
Crabtree Publishing Company

Editors: Leslie Jenkins, Janet Sweet, Lynn Perrigo, Lynn Peppas

Proofreaders: Lisa Slone, Kelly McNiven

Editorial director: Kathy Middleton

Production coordinator: Shivi Sharma

Creative director: Amir Abbasi

Cover design: Samara Parent and Margaret Salter

Photo research: Nivisha Sinha

Maps: Paul Brinkdopke

Production coordinator and prepress technician: Samara Parent

Print coordinator: Katherine Berti

Written, developed, and produced by Planman Technologies

Cover: General George Washington in a painting by Rembrandt Peale entitled *Washington Before Yorktown*.

Title page: (Main): George Washington on horseback leads his soldiers during the battle of Monongahela.
(bottom) Illustration of General Washington on his way to his inauguration as presiednt

Photographs and Reproductions

Front Cover: Library of Congress (b), Shutterstock (t); Title Page: Library of Congress; Table of Content: Library of Congress; Library of Congress; ©ClassicStock / Alamy / IndiaPicture; Library of Congress; McClatchy-Tribune / MCT via Getty Images; Library of Congress; Introduction: Library of Congress; Chapter 1: Library of Congress; Chapter 2: Library of Congress; Chapter 3: Library of Congress; Chapter 4: Library of Congress; Chapter 5: Library of Congress; Page 4: Library of Congress; Page 5: Library of Congress; Page 9: Library of Congress; Page 10: ©Archive Images / Alamy / IndiaPicture; Page 12: ©Ivy Close Images / Alamy / IndiaPicture; Page 13: ©IllustrationCollection / Alamy / IndiaPicture; Page 14: Library of Congress (t); Library of Congress (b); Page 17: ©ClassicStock / Alamy / IndiaPicture (t); Jackson Walker / The National Guard (b); Page 19: Universal / IndiaPicture (t); ©Classic Image / Alamy / IndiaPicture (b); Page 22: Library of Congress; Page 23: Library of Congress; Page 24: Library of Congress; Page 25: Library of Congress; Page 26: Library of Congress; Page 27: Library of Congress; Page 28: Library of Congress; Page 29: Library of Congress; Page 33: Library of Congress; Page 34: Kean Collection / Archive Photos / Getty Images; Page 37: MCT / McClatchy-Tribune / MCT via Getty Images; Page 39: Library of Congress; Page 40: Library of Congress; Page 41: Library of Congress (t); Bill Ragan / Shutterstock (b); (t = top, b = bottom, l = left, c = center, r = right, bkgd = background, fgd = foreground)

Library and Archives Canada Cataloguing in Publication

Aloian, Molly
George Washington : hero of the American Revolution / Molly Aloian.

(Understanding the American Revolution)
Includes bibliographical references and index.
Issued also in electronic format.
ISBN 978-0-7787-0799-8 (bound).--ISBN 978-0-7787-0810-0 (pbk.)

1. Washington, George, 1732-1799--Juvenile literature. 2. United States--History--Revolution, 1775-1783--Juvenile literature. 3. Presidents--United States--Biography--Juvenile literature. I. Title. II. Series: Understanding the American Revolution (St. Catharines, Ont.)

E312.66.A56 2013   j973.4'1092   C2013-900204-9

Library of Congress Cataloging-in-Publication Data

CIP available at Library of Congress

Crabtree Publishing Company

www.crabtreebooks.com   1-800-387-7650

Printed in Canada/022013/BF20130114

Published in Canada
Crabtree Publishing
616 Welland Ave.
St. Catharines, Ontario
L2M 5V6

Published in the United States
Crabtree Publishing
PMB 59051
350 Fifth Avenue, 59th Floor
New York, New York 10118

Published in the United Kingdom
Crabtree Publishing
Maritime House
Basin Road North, Hove
BN41 1WR

Published in Australia
Crabtree Publishing
3 Charles Street
Coburg North
VIC 3058

TABLE *of* CONTENTS

Introduction

The American Revolution was one of the most important events in American history. It was a war between the 13 British **colonies** in North America and the country of Great Britain. The war began in 1775 and went on until 1783. Many factors caused the war, and there were several major battles and brave military leaders. The American general and politician George Washington was one of those leaders.

Thirteen Colonies

The first British colonists reached North America in 1607. They settled in a place they named Jamestown, which is in present-day Virginia. They set up colonies, each with its own governor and local government. In most colonies, the governor had to be approved by King George III. When the American Revolution began in 1775, the United States was divided into 13 colonies. Britain owned and controlled these colonies.

What Do You Know!

ABOUT THE COLONIES

During the American Revolution, the 13 colonies were divided into the New England colonies, the Middle colonies, and the Southern colonies. Many colonists were from Britain, but others were from France, Germany, Holland, and other European countries. There were also slaves living in the 13 colonies. These enslaved people were brought from Africa to America against their will on slave ships. They were forced to become slaves and work for the colonists. Many slaves lived and worked on large farms called plantations.

George Washington (in the black suit) is shown with slaves working at Mount Vernon, his Virginia home.

Britain has the Final Say

People from Europe—many from Britain—sailed across the Atlantic Ocean to start new lives and claim land in the 13 colonies. They were drawn to America's many valuable **natural resources**, including trees, rich soil, and wildlife. The British government had the final say on all aspects of life in the colonies. It enforced laws and created taxes to increase its control over the colonies. Eventually, the colonists wanted **independence** from Britain.

American Victory

During the American Revolution, the American troops managed to win important victories, which eventually led to an **alliance** with France. After a clear British defeat at Yorktown in 1781, a peace treaty was signed in 1783, eight years after the conflict began. After many long years of hardship and war, the colonies officially secured their independence from Great Britain.

General George Washington led the American colonies to victory over Great Britain.

« *The injuries we have received from the British Nation were so **unprovoked**— have been so great and so many, that they can never be forgotten.*

—George Washington, in a letter to John Banister, April 21, 1778 »

Hudson's Bay Company

Nova Scotia

Province of Quebec

Massachusetts

claimed by New York and New Hampshire

New Hampshire

Boston

Massachusetts

New York

Rhode Island
Connecticut

Pennsylvania

New York

New Jersey

Philadelphia

Baltimore

Delaware

Maryland

Virginia

Indian Reserve

Spanish Louisiana

North Carolina

South Carolina

Georgia

Charleston

ATLANTIC OCEAN

West Florida

East Florida

Gulf of Mexico

	British Territory
	Thirteen Colonies (British)
	Spanish Territory
●	major city
- - -	Proclamation Line of 1763*

0 125 250 miles
0 125 250 kilometers

*This line shows the farthest west British settlers were allowed to go. The rest of the land was reserved for Native Americans.

British Colonies before the Revolutionary War

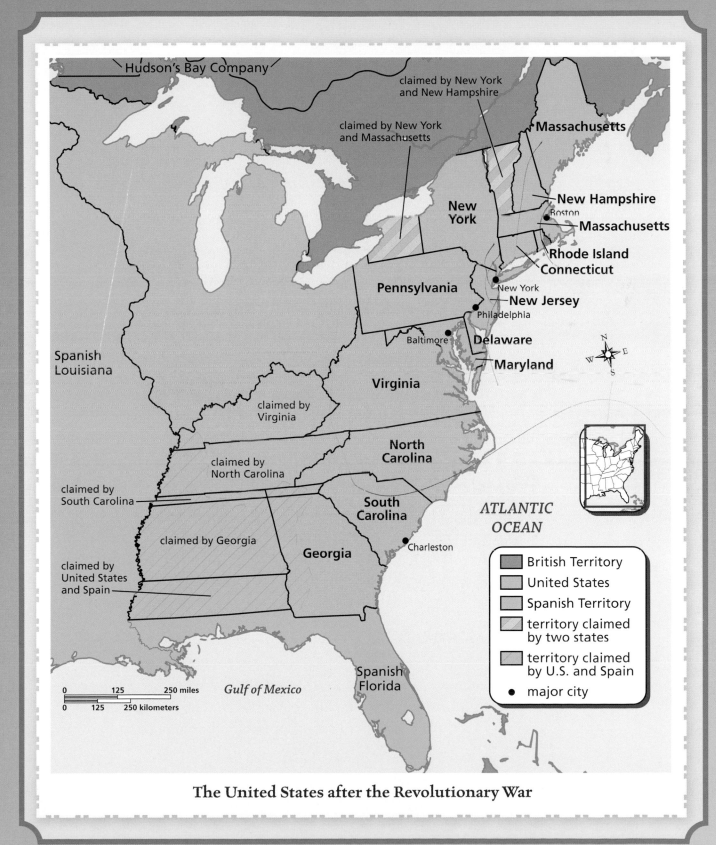

Hudson's Bay Company

claimed by New York
and New Hampshire

claimed by New York
and Massachusetts

Massachusetts

New York

New Hampshire

Boston
Massachusetts

Rhode Island
Connecticut

Pennsylvania

New York
New Jersey

Philadelphia

Baltimore
Delaware

Maryland

Spanish
Louisiana

Virginia

claimed by
Virginia

claimed by
North Carolina

North
Carolina

claimed by
South Carolina

claimed by Georgia

South
Carolina

Charleston

claimed by
United States
and Spain

Georgia

ATLANTIC
OCEAN

N
W   E
S

0   125   250 miles
0   125   250 kilometers

Gulf of Mexico

Spanish
Florida

	British Territory
	United States
	Spanish Territory
	territory claimed by two states
	territory claimed by U.S. and Spain
•	major city

The United States after the Revolutionary War

The Early Years

George Washington was born on February 22, 1732, in Westmoreland County in Virginia. He was the oldest son from his father's second marriage, and he grew up admiring his older half-brother, Lawrence. Under Lawrence's careful guidance, George learned how to become an exceptional leader. This quality would be invaluable to him in his career.

Washington's Ancestors Arrive in America

The first English settlement in America was founded at Jamestown, Virginia, in 1607. The Virginia Company was in charge of the colony until 1624, when it became a royal colony. The colony was under royal control when George Washington's ancestors arrived.

George Washington's family came from Essex, in eastern England. In 1657, his great-grandfather, John Washington, traveled from England to Virginia to start a new life. Upon his arrival, John stayed with a plantation owner named Nathaniel Pope. He fell in love with Pope's daughter, Anne, and married her. As a wedding gift, Pope gave them over a square mile (3 sq. km) of **fertile** land in Westmoreland County. Soon after, John became a successful tobacco plantation owner. He owned slaves, who tended his tobacco crops.

House of Burgesses

John Washington was the first Washington to become a politician in North America. He was selected for the **House of Burgesses** in Virginia and became a politician in the colony. The House of Burgesses was the first colonial government in North America. It was set up in Virginia in 1619, and each settlement in the colony originally had two representatives. During this time, most of the other colonies had created their own governments, known as **assemblies**. Male property owners elected the members of the assemblies.

The head of colonial governments were governors. The governor had a council that he appointed. Some colonies, such as in New England, had town meetings instead of a governor's council. Oftentimes, the colonial assembly would pass laws, the governor's council would approve them, and the governor would carry them out. This structure can be seen today in the United States Congress and presidency.

Growing Wealth

Within 20 years, John Washington owned more than 5,000 acres (2,000 hectares) of land. His sons and grandsons continued to purchase land and increase their wealth. The Washington family was highly respected within colonial America.

Augustine Washington, John's grandson and George's father, had two wives. Augustine and his first wife, Jane Butler, had four children. Two years after Jane's death in 1729, Augustine married Mary Ball. George was the first of six children from that second marriage. In 1738, Augustine moved his family from their large plantation—known today as Mount Vernon—to Ferry Farm near Fredericksburg, Virginia.

Mary Ball Washington

Wakefield

In 1717 or 1718, Augustine Washington bought land facing Popes Creek, which was about one mile (2 km) southeast of his home on Bridges Creek. From 1722 to 1726, Augustine built the home that became known as Wakefield on this tract of land. He and his family soon moved in. In late 1729, his first wife Jane died at Wakefield. He remarried two years later and brought his second wife, Mary, to live at Wakefield.

Slave Society

Augustine was a wealthy man who **acquired** not only land, but also slaves. During the early 1700s, wealthy landowners in Virginia and other Southern Colonies relied heavily on slaves. Slaves were very important to the Southern Colonies and their **economy**. Slaves had no rights and were not paid for their work. Colonists bought and sold slaves like property. They were often traded for other kinds of goods and services. Slaves were also used to pay off outstanding debts. When calculating the value of estates, the estimated value of each slave was included. This became the source of tax revenue for local and state governments.

> " *To Be Sold; A Parcel of likely Negroes, imported from Africa, cheap for cash, or short credit.*
>
> —an advertisement in the *Boston Evening Post,* August 3, 1761 "

Slaves working on a cotton plantation.

Early Childhood

In 1743, when George was just 11 years old, his father died. George's 25-year-old half-brother, Lawrence, stepped in and became like a father to George. Lawrence had gone to a well-known school in England, and George admired his intelligence and gentlemanly manners.

Lawrence inherited Mount Vernon and made his home there. He married Anne Fairfax, who was related to Lord Thomas Fairfax, the wealthiest landowner in Virginia. Through Lord Fairfax, Lawrence introduced George to many influential landowners and politicians. Although George lived mainly with his mother at Ferry Farm, he visited Lawrence and Anne at Mount Vernon as often as he could.

Self-Taught

A variety of tutors taught George practical math, geography, Latin, and the English classics, but George did not receive as fine of an education as Lawrence. George was in his mid-teens when he began teaching himself how to measure and map land. This was called **surveying**. Surveying allowed George to make good use of his math skills. Anne and Lawrence also taught him about gentlemanly manners and instructed him on how to fit in with the wealthy and cultured people of the colonies.

> *My mother was the most beautiful woman I ever saw. All I am I owe to my mother. I attribute all my success in life to the moral, intellectual and physical education I received from her.*
>
> —George Washington

What Do You Know!

George desperately wanted to join the British navy, but he could not do so without his mother's permission. He never joined because his mother was overly fearful about her children's health and well-being.

People in the War

Mary Ball Washington

Historians do not know the exact date of Mary Ball's birth, but they believe she was born in 1708 in Virginia. By the time she was 12 years old, both Mary's mother and father had died. A lawyer named George Eskridge became her guardian. She married Augustine Washington on March 6, 1731. It was Augustine's second marriage and Mary's first. In 1732, Mary gave birth to her first son, George, who was named after George Eskridge.

Getting Hired

During one of his many visits to Mount Vernon, George met the wealthy Lord Fairfax. Lord Fairfax owned more than 5 million acres (2 million hectares) of land in Virginia, and he hired George to help survey his land beyond the Blue Ridge Mountains. This allowed George to explore the wilderness frontier of Virginia and become familiar with its landmarks. It also enabled him to find and purchase available pieces of land that he liked.

Surveying was difficult work that required both skill and honesty. Since young George was good in mathematics, had neat penmanship, and made accurate maps, he adapted well to his new profession. By the age of 17, George was a successful, highly skilled land surveyor. He was well-known for being honest, exact, methodical, and complete.

George Washington as a surveyor.

A Skilled Surveyor

In 1748, when he was 16, George traveled with a surveying group that was mapping land in western Virginia. He loved exploring the wild land and meeting the **indigenous**, or native, people who had been living there long before Europeans arrived in the area. The next year, with Lord Fairfax's help, George became the official surveyor for Culpepper County, Virginia. George surveyed the land in Culpepper, Frederick, and Augusta counties for the next two years. The time spent plotting the rugged landscape strengthened George's mind and body. His familiarity with the land and physical strength would also come in handy later on during his military career.

Disease and Death

By 1751, Lawrence was suffering from a lung disease called **tuberculosis**. He took George on a voyage to the island of Barbados in the hopes that the warmer climate would improve his health. George caught **smallpox** during the trip. He recovered, although the disease left some scars on his face. Lawrence's condition continued to deteriorate, so they returned to Mount Vernon. Lawrence died in June 1752 at the age of 34.

Heir Apparent

Lawrence and Anne's only child, Sarah, died just two years after Lawrence. Without a son or daughter to inherit the Washington lands, Anne deeded Mount Vernon to George. At just 20 years old, George had inherited one of Virginia's most **prominent** estates. He was well on his way to becoming one of the wealthier property owners in the colony. George's experience of running the large estate and managing its workers would prove valuable to him later in life as commander of the Continental Army.

> **What Do You Think?**
>
> How did Lawrence's influence help shape George Washington's life? Would it have made a difference if George had gone to a well-known school like Lawrence did?

NATIVE AMERICANS OF VIRGINIA

Native Americans had been living in Virginia and throughout the rest of North America for thousands of years before any European colonists arrived. Native Americans lived in villages they had established in different territories throughout the region. They hunted animals in the forests and fished in the many waterways in the area. During the summer and early fall, many Native Americans harvested crops, such as corn, beans, squash, pumpkins, and sunflowers. The arrival of European colonists had devastating effects on the lives of Native Americans, and there were many violent conflicts over tracts of lands.

Powhatan, the leader of Native Americans in Virginia who came in contact with English settlers at Jamestown, said this:

Chief Powhatan as seen by the British.

> "
> *Why will you take by force what you may obtain by love? Why will you destroy us who supply you with food? What can you get by war? . . . We are unarmed, and willing to give you what you ask, if you come in a friendly manner. . .*
> "
>
> —Chief Powhatan, chief of the Native Americans in Virginia, 1609

This is a painting of the marriage of George Washington and Martha Dandridge Custis, January 6, 1759.

Married to Martha

In 1758, George met and fell in love with a young, beautiful, and wealthy widow named Martha Dandridge Custis. Martha had two children from her previous marriage. Her son John was six years old and her daughter Martha was four years old. George adored both of the children and was heartbroken when young Martha died just before the American Revolution began.

Martha had an 18,000-acre (7,000-hectare) estate, from which George personally acquired 6,000 acres (2 hectares) of land. The marriage greatly increased George's land holdings, making him one of the wealthiest landowners in Virginia. On January 6, 1759, George and Martha married. They were married for nearly 40 years, but had no children together.

> *The greater part of our happiness or misery depends upon our dispositions, and not our upon circumstances.*
>
> —Martha Dandridge Custis Washington

What Do You Know!

Following his marriage to Martha, George settled into life at Mount Vernon as a farmer. He raised hogs and learned about growing crops, including tobacco, corn, and wheat. He also enjoyed hunting and fishing.

George and Martha Washington's home, which was called Mount Vernon.

Early Military Pursuits

Washington built a career in the military fighting in conflicts during the French and Indian War. In 1758, he was elected to Virginia's House of Burgesses.

Land Wars

In the 1750s, life in the colonies was not always peaceful. The British, French, and Native Americans were constantly fighting over land in North America. In the early 1750s, France and Britain were at peace, but this did not last long. The French military began taking over much of the Ohio Valley. In October 1753, Virginia's lieutenant governor, Robert Dinwiddie, found out that the French military was building forts there. He decided to send them a letter of warning and chose George Washington to deliver it.

Words of Warning

On Dinwiddie's order, Washington traveled to Fort LeBoeuf—in present-day Waterford, Pennsylvania—to command the French to abandon all of their forts that were sitting on British territory between Lake Ontario and the Ohio River. The French refused. Washington quickly returned to the colonial capital of Williamsburg only to find out that Dinwiddie was sending him back—this time with troops. Washington and his troops set up a post at Great Meadows called Fort Necessity, and prepared for an attack on the French.

Major Events

1753

October
George becomes a major in the Virginia **militia**

1754

French and Indian War begins

1755

February
George is sent to serve as an assistant and advisor to General Edward Braddock

July 13
General Braddock is mortally wounded during an ambush

August
George is appointed commander of all Virginia militia forces

1758

George resigns as commander of the Virginia forces

⟡ What Do You Know!

The French and Indian War is so named because both the French and the British had formed alliances with Native Americans during the war. In Canada and Europe, the French and Indian War is often called the Seven Years' War.

The French and Indian War Begins

In July 1754, Washington's troops attacked the French at Fort Duquesne. They killed the commander, Joseph Coulon de Jumonville, nine other men, and took the rest as prisoners. This was one of the events that marked the beginning of the French and Indian War. The French counterattacked and drove Washington and his small force back to his post at Great Meadows. The French and their Native American allies outnumbered Washington's troops—one-quarter of his men were quickly killed or wounded—and forced Washington to **surrender**. He surrendered on the condition that he could lead his men home.

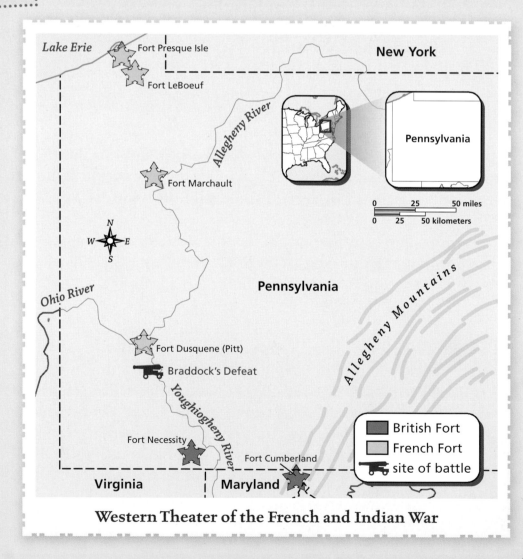

Western Theater of the French and Indian War

Colonel Washington

Superior officers were quick to recognize Washington's careful planning and tactics during the attack on the French. Washington was considered a hero even though he surrendered to the French. He ensured his troops were led to safety, which showed bravery and determination. Despite his defeat, the House of Burgesses **commended** Washington for his efforts against the French. He was promoted to colonel and was put in command of a small army of Virginia and North Carolina troops and Native American allies.

George Washington on his journey to the French forts during the French and Indian War

The rank of colonel was the third rank Washington had held in four years. He was appointed as a major in 1753 by Robert Dinwiddie. Washington was quickly promoted to lieutenant colonel in 1754. In 1755, Washington was promoted yet again, this time to colonel. The next rank Washington would hold was major general of the Continental Forces in 1775.

Some Native American nations fought against the British during the French and Indian War. Other groups were British allies, fighting alongside George Washington's troops.

George Washington, Tanacharison, and the Iroquois Confederacy

On his way to warn the French to leave their forts, Washington met a Native American leader called Tanacharison (Tanaghrisson). Washington and Tanacharison, who was known to Europeans as Half King, became friends and allies. Tanacharison lived in a village about 20 miles (32 km) downstream from the Ohio River. He acted as Washington's guide to Fort LeBoeuf and was a spokesperson for the Native American peoples of Ohio. It is believed that Tanacharison was born into the Catawba nation, taken captive by the French, and later adopted into the Seneca nation. The Seneca were one of the six nations of the Iroquois Confederacy. These six nations in the confederacy shared language similarities, followed a positive code of values, and lived together in peace.

> *Fathers, both you and the English are white, we live in a Country between; therefore the Land belongs to neither one nor to other; But the Great Being Above allow'd it to be a Place of Residence for us; so Fathers, I desire you to withdraw, as I have done our Brothers the English; for I will keep you at Arms length. I lay this down as a Trial for both, to see which will have the greatest Regard to it, and that Side we will stand by, and make equal Sharers with us.*
>
> —Tanacharison (Tanaghrisson), to the commander of a French fort in the Ohio valley, November 25, 1753

Before the founding of the Iroquois Confederacy, the six Native American nations fought wars against each other. According to the history of the Iroquois, a leader—called the Peacemaker—went to the nations with a message of peace and unity. He persuaded each nation to accept the Great Law of Peace, which detailed clear rules and procedures for making decisions through representatives and consensus. By following the Great Law of Peace, the nations established a common government, the Iroquois Confederacy, that allowed them to work together and respect each other.

George and General Braddock

In February 1755, Washington was sent to serve as an assistant and adviser to the British general named Edward Braddock. The British planned to attack three French forts—Fort Duquesne, Fort Niagara, and Crown Point. The military goal behind this British **strategy**, known as the Braddock Expedition, was to remove the French from the Ohio Valley once and for all. Washington was eager to learn from General Braddock and Braddock respected Washington's bravery and leadership skills. He even listened to Washington's opinions and advice on military strategies.

Braddock's Defeat

On July 9, 1755, the French and their Native American allies ambushed Braddock and shot him off his horse. Braddock was seriously wounded and died within days. The British soldiers fought bravely against the French, but there was no one to organize the troops and many British soldiers were killed. In the midst of the devastating **casualties** and **chaos**, Washington stepped in and maintained some order. He rallied the British troops into an organized **retreat**. Braddock's defeat was a major blow for the British in the early stages of the war with France.

People in the War

General Braddock

Edward Braddock was born in 1695 and entered the British army in 1710. After 45 years of rising through the military ranks, Braddock became commander in chief of all the British forces in North America. In February 1755, he arrived in Virginia to join forces with American generals and to take back Fort Duquesne for Britain and America.

> " *[General Braddock] was, I think, a brave man, and might probably have made a figure as a good officer in some European war. But he had too much self-confidence, too high an opinion of the validity of regular troops, and too mean a one of both Americans and Indians.* "
>
> —Benjamin Franklin, describing General Edward Braddock

Major General Braddock's death at the Battle of Monongahela on July 9, 1755.

Patrol and Protect

In August 1755, Lieutenant Governor Dinwiddie made Washington commander of all Virginia militia forces. He was just 23 years old. Washington and his troops were responsible for patrolling and protecting Virginia's 400-mile (644 km) **frontier** border. They built small forts along the frontier, but **settlers** in townships nearby feared for their lives.

Life on the Virginia frontier in the mid-1700s was very difficult. Families would often live in rough log cabins that were cold in the winter and warm in the summer. Families would spend the spring, summer, and autumn growing food and raising livestock to keep themselves fed. In the winter, particularly in mountainous areas, there was little to do and little to eat. For many, the hardest time of the year was in the early spring when the winter stores had run out, but before trees and bushes bloomed with berries. Townships were far apart, and travel between them was difficult for most people. It was not uncommon for news to take months to reach the frontier from the coastal cities.

Forbes Expedition

After getting sick with **dysentery** in 1757, Washington went home to rest. When he returned to duty, another **expedition** was organized to capture Fort Duquesne. In 1758, Washington participated in the Forbes Expedition with British General John Forbes. The expedition attacked Fort Duquesne once again, but the French and their allies killed 14 and wounded 26 of Washington's men. Ultimately, the British finally gained control of the Ohio Valley, when the French burned and abandoned the fort. Forbes then built Fort Pitt on the site. In 1758, Washington resigned from commanding the Virginia forces with the **honorary rank** of brigadier general. While he was serving in the Forbes Expedition, Washington was elected to the Virginia House of Burgesses. His career in politics had just begun.

3 Leadership and the Revolutionary War

For the next several years, George Washington devoted his time and attention to developing his estate, tending to his tobacco and other crops, and managing his livestock. When the Revolutionary War broke out in April 1775, Washington was appointed commander in chief of all colonial military forces.

Opposing Independence?

During the 1760s, many colonists became strongly opposed to British rule. They wanted independence from Britain and had grown tired of obeying laws made by a king who lived an ocean away. Britain also placed harsh taxes on the colonists, who believed it was unfair to be taxed so heavily when they were not even allowed to vote for representatives in their government. Angry colonists used the **slogan**, "No taxation without representation," to protest.

At first, Washington did not want to take the lead in the growing colonial **resistance** against the British. During this time, he wrote letters that revealed that he was completely opposed to the colonies declaring independence.

> " *Taxation without representation is tyranny.* "
>
> —James Otis, American politician from 1725 to 1783

Major Events

1765
March 27
Parliament passes the Stamp Act

1770
March 5
Boston Massacre

1774
The Intolerable Acts are passed

1775
April 19
The Revolutionary War begins

June 15
Washington is appointed major general and commander in chief of the colonial forces

1777
December
Washington **withdraws** his army to Valley Forge

1781
October 19
British troops surrender at Yorktown, Virginia

King George III

Getting Upset

King George III created the Proclamation of 1763 to stop colonists from settling west beyond the Allegheny Mountains. The king did this to ease the Native Americans' fears of being driven out of their territories by the colonists. The proclamation greatly upset Washington. Washington also opposed the Stamp Act of 1763, which forced colonists to pay a tax on every piece of printed paper they used. This included legal papers, newspapers, licenses, and even playing cards. He believed these were major violations of the rights of colonists. In 1769, Washington took a stand and introduced a resolution to the House of Burgesses. He asked Virginia to **boycott** British goods until the acts were **repealed**.

Massacre in Boston

The Boston Massacre was a violent incident that took place on March 5, 1770, between colonists and British soldiers in Boston, Massachusetts. British troops had been in Boston for almost two years by the winter of 1770, and tensions were high between local men and British soldiers. A group of unruly Bostonians began throwing snowballs at a British guard. Noticing the **skirmish**, more soldiers came to help the guard. Shots were fired, and shortly thereafter several people lay wounded, dying, or dead in the snow. The exact details about who fired the shots remained unclear, but the Boston Massacre showed both the colonists and the British that tensions had reached a dangerous new level.

The Intolerable Acts

In 1774, the Intolerable Acts were passed. These were a series of laws put forth by the British prime minister, Lord North. They were designed to discourage American rebellion and keep the colonists under British rule. The acts backfired, however, and only sparked more opposition.

Following the passage of the Intolerable Acts, Washington chaired a meeting to adopt the Fairfax Resolves. This set of **resolutions** rejected Britain's royal authority in the American colonies and called for a gathering of the Continental Congress. Washington was selected to be a delegate to the First Continental Congress in March 1775. Many of the members of the Continental Congress wanted independence from Britain.

What Do You Think?

Do you think the early Americans were right to fight against British taxes? Why or why not?

🌠 The Boston Tea Party

In the 1700s, tea was a very popular beverage in both England and colonial America. Almost all the tea that the colonists drank came from British sources, such as the East India Company. Many colonists resented the tax they had to pay for tea, viewing it as another unfair act by the British government. On the night of December 17, 1773, a group of colonists disguised themselves as Native Americans and slipped aboard the tea ships that were anchored in Boston Harbor. They threw hundreds of chests of tea into the water. This act of protest, known as the Boston Tea Party, destroyed nearly 90,000 pounds (41,000 kg) of tea, worth about $1 million in today's currency.

Supporting the War

The Revolutionary War began near Boston with the Battles of Lexington and Concord on April 19, 1775. In May 1775, Washington attended the Second Continental Congress dressed in a military uniform. This was a clear sign that he was prepared to participate in the war. He was not yet totally in favor of independence, but he was still willing to engage in armed conflict against British rule in the colonies.

On June 15, 1775, he was appointed major general and commander in chief of the colonial forces against Great Britain. Congress had created the Continental Army just one day earlier. Washington had been advising Congress for months, and his leadership skills and military experience made him the perfect man for the job.

Lacking Experience

At that time, Britain was the world's most powerful nation with the best-trained, best-equipped army. Washington was not qualified to lead a war against such a **superpower**. His military training and experience was mainly in frontier warfare, which consisted of small numbers of soldiers. He had little to no training in the open-field style of battle that

George Washington as commander in chief of the Continental Army.

was familiar to the British generals. He also had no experience in organizing, providing supplies for, or leading such large groups of cavalry and infantry. It was his courage, intelligence, and sheer determination that allowed him to keep one step ahead of the British.

> *Discipline is the soul of an army. It makes small numbers* **formidable**; *procures success to the weak and esteem to all.*
>
> —George Washington, in a letter to the captains of the Virginia regiments, July 29, 1759

Other Hardships

Washington faced other hardships as well. **Desertion** was a frequent problem since American soldiers were poorly paid for their duties. They were also not well-trained. Even the officers frequently fought with one another. Washington maintained discipline by punishing deserters and encouraging a sense of **patriotism** among his troops. In an attempt to maintain the welfare of his army, Washington asked the Continental Congress for better pay and more food rations.

> *Remember officers and soldiers, that you are free men, fighting for the blessings of liberty—that slavery will be your portion, and that of your posterity, if you do not acquit yourselves like men.*
>
> —George Washington, 1776

Battle of Lexington

> *These are the times that try men's souls.*
>
> —Thomas Paine, writer and member of the colonial army December 23, 1776

Boston to New York

In March 1776, Washington and his small army had an early victory in Boston. They placed powerful cannons on Dorchester Heights, which was an area of low hills overlooking Boston and its harbor, and prepared to attack the city. The action forced the British to leave the area. Washington then moved his troops into New York City to take advantage of the city's importance as a naval base and its **accessibility** to the Hudson River. He spread about 20,000 soldiers along the shores of New York's harbor, mainly on Long Island and Manhattan.

Washington leads Patriot troops in New York.

Retreat from New York

In June, however, the new British general named William Howe arrived in the colonies with the largest army Britain had ever **deployed**. In August 1776, the British army attacked and quickly took over New York City. They drove the colonists back to Brooklyn Heights, which was a great victory for Britain. Often called the Battle of Long Island, this was the largest battle of the Revolutionary War. Eventually, Washington withdrew his entire remaining army across the Delaware River into Pennsylvania.

General Sir William Howe

Hessians under Attack

General Howe's troops spent the winter at Trenton and Princeton, New Jersey. German soldiers—called **Hessians**—were hired by Britain to protect the British fort at Trenton. On Christmas night in 1776, Washington and his men crossed the Delaware River and ambushed the Hessians. Taken by surprise in the middle of the night, the Hessians were caught unprepared and forced to surrender. A few days later, the colonial army attacked the British again, this time at Princeton, which led to another humiliating British defeat.

Losses in Pennsylvania

In the fall of 1777, Washington and the colonial army suffered losses against the British in Pennsylvania. During the Battle of Brandywine, the British defeated the Americans and forced them to withdraw to Philadelphia. The British also won the Battle of Germantown. In December 1777, Washington withdrew his army to a military camp called Valley Forge in Pennsylvania. That winter was extremely harsh and difficult at Valley Forge. Nearly 2,000 of Washington's men died from disease and exposure to bitterly cold weather.

Hessian soldiers fighting for Britain.

> "Men are confined in hospitals or in farmers' houses for want of shoes. We have this day [December 23] no less than 2,873 men in camp unfit for duty because they are barefooted and otherwise naked. Our whole strength in Continental troops amounts to no more than 8,200 in camp fit for duty. Since the 4th inst., our numbers fit for duty, from hardships and exposures, have decreased nearly 2,000 men. Numbers are still obliged to sit all night by fires. Gentlemen [condemn] going into winter-quarters as much as if they thought the soldiers were made of sticks or stones. I can assure those gentlemen that it is a much easier and less distressing thing to draw [complaints] in a comfortable room by a good fireside than to occupy a cold, bleak hill, and sleep under frost and snow without clothes or blankets. However, although they seem to have little feeling for the naked and distressed soldiers, I feel superabundantly for them; and from my soul I pity those miseries which it is neither in my power to relieve nor prevent."
>
> —George Washington, December 23, 1777

France Steps In

The summer of 1778 was an important one in the colonies. France recognized the colonies as an independent nation and sent military support to help Washington's forces battle the British. They sent ships and soldiers, which gave the colonists the courage to keep fighting. The British then began taking over the Southern Colonies. They captured Savannah and Augusta in Georgia and Charleston, South Carolina. By the summer of 1780, the British had captured much of the South.

Washington and his French allies decided to attack British General Lord Charles Cornwallis's troops at Yorktown, Virginia, in the Battle of Yorktown. The American troops greatly outnumbered the British troops. French ships arrived to prevent the British from escaping by water or getting more reinforcements. Washington had no idea at the time, but the attack at Yorktown was the move that would end the war. On October 19, 1781, Cornwallis surrendered his forces.

Valley Forge

Resigning from the Army

After British troops surrendered to the Continental Army at Yorktown, Virginia, peace talks began in Paris, France. On September 3, 1783, an agreement called the Treaty of Paris ended the American Revolution. The war was essentially over. The colonists had finally won their independence and the United States of America was born. By November of 1783, the British had left New York and other cities. Washington said goodbye to his troops and on December 23, 1783, he resigned as commander in chief of the army. He returned home to Mount Vernon. Although he had proved to be an excellent military leader, Washington most of all wanted "to see this plague of mankind, war, banished from the earth."

> *The United States in Congress assembled, after giving the most honorable testimony to the Merits of the Federal Armies, and presenting them with the thanks of their Country for their long, eminent and faithful Services, having thought proper, by their Proclamation bearing date the 18th day of October last, to discharge such part of the Troops as were engaged for the War, and to permit the Officers on Furlough to retire from Service from and after tomorrow, which Proclamation having been communicated in the public papers for the information and government of all concerned. it only remains for the Commander in Chief to address himself once more, and that for the last time, to the Armies of the United States (however widely dispersed the Individuals who composed them may be) and to bid them an affectionate—a long farewell.*
>
> —George Washington's farewell orders issued to the armies of the United States of America

Mr. President

George Washington spent the next few years enjoying a more peaceful life at Mount Vernon, but he was called to serve his country once again in 1787. America had won its independence, but the states were fighting over land and were not **unified** at all. The country needed guidance and a new constitution. On February 4, 1789, Washington became the first president of the United States.

Unstable Government

American citizens all knew that something needed to be done to improve America's government. Since its independence, the new country had been struggling under the Articles of Confederation, a plan of government that **equalized** power among the states. The states were fighting over land boundaries and navigation rights. They were also refusing to help pay off the nation's war debts.

The Constitutional Convention

In 1787, Washington was chosen to preside over the Constitutional Convention in Philadelphia, Pennsylvania. The convention took place from May 25, 1787, to September 17, 1787, with the goal of resolving America's problems. By July 1788, a new constitution was drafted. Eleven of the 13 states **ratified** the new U.S. Constitution, making it the supreme law in the United States of America.

Major Events

1787

May 25
George Washington presides over the Constitutional Convention

1789

February 4
George Washington becomes the first president of the United States

1791

December 15
Congress passes the Bill of Rights

1793

April 22
George Washington issues the Proclamation of Neutrality

President of the United States

On February 4, 1789, George Washington received all 69 electoral votes and he was **unanimously** elected as president of the United States. To this day, he is still the only president to have received 100 percent of the electoral votes. He was **inaugurated** into office on April 30, 1789, and took the oath of office on the balcony at Federal Hall in New York City, which was the capital of the United States during that time. John Adams was elected vice president. By 1790, the remaining two states, North Carolina and Rhode Island, had also ratified the Constitution, and Congress was the governing body of the United States.

First in Line

Being the first president of the United States was an enormous undertaking. Washington and his Congress faced many complicated challenges, the biggest of which was putting the Constitution into practice. Congress and state governments had piled up huge debts paying for the war. Some Americans agreed when Congress began to raise money through taxes. Other Americans strongly disagreed. Washington carefully attended to the responsibilities and duties of his office. He was especially careful not to follow the traditions of any European royal court. He chose the title "Mr. President" instead of the grander titles others suggested.

Washington initially declined the $25,000 salary Congress offered him as president. In Washington's mind, he was already wealthy and wanted to maintain his image as an unselfish servant to the public. Congress eventually convinced him to accept the salary to avoid giving the impression that only wealthy men could be president of the United States.

🎇 What is the Oath of Office?

The oath of office of the president of the United States is a solemn promise required by the United States Constitution before the president begins his duties. The wording of the oath is found in the Constitution: "I do solemnly swear [or affirm] that I will faithfully execute the Office of President of the United States, and will to the best of my Ability, preserve, protect and defend the Constitution of the United States." Robert Livingston, the chancellor of New York in 1789, administered the oath of office to George Washington.

Inauguration of George Washington

Uniting the Nation

Washington knew that any decisions he made or policies that he began would likely become the model for other presidents in the years to come. He traveled all over the country and worked hard to unite the nation. He even listened to the thoughts and opinions of everyday citizens. He was determined to make the United States a powerful and respected nation throughout the world. He firmly believed that the United States must insist on its national identity, strength, and dignity.

"
*I walk on untrodden ground. . . . There is scarcely any part of my conduct which may not hereafter be drawn into **precedent***.
—George Washington, 1789
"

Debts and Taxes

During Washington's time as president, the power and influence of the federal government was greatly strengthened. People were slowly getting used to a government without a king. In 1791, George Washington and Alexander Hamilton **chartered** the Bank of the United States, and the new government took responsibility for both national and state debts. The government placed taxes on imported goods and on some private property within the states. Money was deposited into the **national treasury** for paying debts.

Whiskey Rebellion

In 1791, Washington also signed a bill that allowed Congress to tax **distilled** liquor. This caused huge protests in rural areas of Pennsylvania because many poor farmers distilled their own whiskey. The liquor was easier to transport and sell than the grain from which it was made. The protests worked up into a full-blown rebellion known as the Whiskey Rebellion. Washington **invoked** the Militia Act of 1792, calling on local militias from several states to stop the rebellion. Washington personally marched the troops into the areas of rebellion to show that the federal government was prepared to use force when needed to uphold the law.

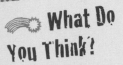

What Do You Think?

How do you think Washington's time in office influenced later presidents? Do you think his ideals should still be applied today?

Farmers attacked tax collectors during the Whiskey Rebellion. Some tax collectors were even tarred and feathered. Farmers felt that the tax on distilled liquor was unfair.

Bill of Rights

Congress passed the Bill of Rights on December 15, 1791. The Bill of Rights is the name for the first ten **amendments** to the Constitution. James Madison introduced the amendments to Congress as a series of **legislative** articles. They **ensured** the personal rights and freedoms of individual Americans and protected the natural rights of liberty and property. They were designed to limit the government's power and grant some power to the states and the public.

What Do You Know!

As a national figure, Washington was obligated to offer hospitality to old army friends, visitors from other states and nations, diplomats, and delegations of Native Americans. As a result, he and Martha Washington seldom sat down to dinner alone.

Neutral in Foreign Affairs

In 1793, when war broke out between France and Great Britain, Washington refused the recommendations of his Secretary of State, Thomas Jefferson, who supported France, and his Secretary of the Treasury, Alexander Hamilton, who supported Great Britain. He insisted on remaining **neutral** in **foreign affairs** until the United States had a chance to grow stronger and increase its stability. Even though the United States owed France for the help during the American Revolution—America actually promised to help France in any future conflicts—Washington believed that the United States was not prepared to enter another war so soon. In April 1793, he issued the Proclamation of Neutrality. It stated that the United States must maintain a sense of national identity, separate from any other country's influence.

> *My ardent desire is, and my aim has been . . . to comply strictly with all our engagements foreign and domestic; but to keep the United States free from political connections with every other country, to see them independent of all, and under the influence of none. In a word, I want an American character that the powers of Europe may be convinced we act for ourselves and not for others; this, in my judgment, is the only way to be respected abroad and happy at home.*
>
> —George Washington

Federalists and Republicans

Two political parties—the Federalist Party led by Alexander Hamilton and the Republican Party led by Thomas Jefferson—grew during Washington's first year as president. Both parties expressed their views of how the government ought to operate in the new **republic**.

Hamilton's Federalist Party favored the northern businessmen and close ties with Great Britain. Federalists wanted America to convert its farms to cities and industries and believed the wealthy upper class had an automatic right to run the government. Jefferson's Republican Party favored southern farmers and close ties with France. Republicans disliked urban growth and believed "the common man" could be trusted to govern the nation well through their election of qualified representatives.

Washington Stays Neutral

Party lines and loyalty were drawn to the point of personal bitterness and public destructiveness. Washington was determined not to take sides. He viewed political parties as focused on gaining power and revenge to the point of being destructive to the good of the nation. Because of Washington's neutral views, the leaders of both parties begged him to stay on for a second term as president. Jefferson is credited as telling Washington, "North and South will hang together if they have you to hang on."

Only the Best

Meanwhile, Washington's administration received a lot of criticism, as did his leadership and lifestyle. During his two terms as president, he rented only the best houses in both New York and Philadelphia. When the governor of New York offered him a place to stay, Washington refused. He believed that the president of a nation should be no man's guest. He returned no calls and shook hands with no one. He commonly greeted people with formal bows. At receptions and public ceremonies, Washington dressed in a black velvet suit with gold buckles and wore yellow gloves. He had powdered hair and a sword in a white leather sheath.

Private Parties

On Friday afternoons, Martha Washington held formal receptions, at which the president appeared. Washington insisted that these events be private, even though the presidents of the Continental Congress had made their tables somewhat open to the public. Washington served expensive wine and very fancy foods. Some guests, including the senator of Pennsylvania, William Maclay, commented that the atmosphere was too formal and even went so far as to accuse the president of acting like a king. However, Washington was always aware that his conduct would set the precedent for those to follow.

What Do You Know!

When George Washington took the oath of office, he raised his right hand and placed his left hand on a Bible. Today, when new presidents take the oath of office, they do the same thing.

Barack Obama is sworn in as president during his inauguration on January 20, 2009.

5 *Final Days*

Major Events

1796

September 19
George Washington's Farewell Address is published

1797

March 4
George Washington finishes his second term as president of the United States

March 4
John Adams is sworn in as president and Thomas Jefferson as vice president

1799

December 14
George Washington dies in his Mount Vernon home

George Washington finished his second term as president on March 4, 1797. He felt plenty of pressure to take on a third term as president, but he refused. He had led his fellow Americans in war and peace, but he had grown tired of public life and longed to retire at Mount Vernon.

Farewell

Washington bade his country farewell in a letter that is now called Washington's Farewell Address. Washington and Alexander Hamilton wrote the letter to the people of the United States to share Washington's reasons for not accepting a third term in office. Washington believed that it was unwise for one person to hold a position of power for so long.

In his letter, Washington encouraged the United States to concentrate on American interests. He also warned against the rise of political parties because he saw them as a threat to national unity. Washington's Farewell Address was originally published in the *American Daily Advertiser* on September 19, 1796, but was almost immediately reprinted in newspapers across the country and in a special pamphlet.

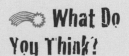

What Do You Think?

Do you agree with Washington that one person should not hold the powerful position of president for more than four years? Why or why not?

Thomas Jefferson

People in the War

Thomas Jefferson

Thomas Jefferson was born on April 13, 1743 at Shadwell, Virginia. He was the main author of the Declaration of Independence and one of America's founding fathers. He was also a politician, diplomat, and plantation owner. He worked hard to make the words in the Declaration of Independence a reality for the people of the United States and eventually became the third president. He died on July 4, 1826, just hours before his close friend, John Adams, died. That date also marked the fiftieth anniversary of the adoption of the Declaration of Independence.

On March 4, 1797, John Adams was sworn in as president of the United States. Thomas Jefferson was the new vice president. This was an important moment in world history. It was a peaceful transition of power from one leader to another. Even more important was the election of 1800 in which Jefferson defeated Adams. The country changed leaders and political parties in a fair election without violence. These early transitions of power left an important precedent for the young United States.

The Simple Life

Washington returned to Mount Vernon in the spring of 1797 with a sense of relief and accomplishment. He left his country at peace, its debts manageable, and its future secure. The country was now in John Adams's capable hands. At Mount Vernon, Washington spent his time managing his farm and entertaining guests and visitors. He looked forward to living his last years as a simple gentleman farmer. In 1798, President John Adams appointed Washington as commander in chief of a **provisional** army after the threat of war with France. The war never happened, however, and Washington never took command.

Grave of George Washington

Death of a President

On a snowy day in December 1799, Washington returned home on horseback after several hours in the cold. He was exhausted, ate his supper early in his wet clothes, and then went to bed. The next morning, he awoke with a severe sore throat and became increasingly ill. The illness progressed until he died late in the evening of December 14, 1799. Some of his last words were "I feel myself going. I thank you for your attentions; but I pray you to take no more trouble about me. Let me go off quietly. I cannot last long." The news of his death spread throughout the United States like wildfire. The entire nation mourned the passing of its first president. Washington was buried in the family vault at Mount Vernon on December 18, 1799.

Forever First

John Marshall, who served under George Washington at Valley Forge, quoted part of a **eulogy** for Washington by the American Revolutionary officer Henry Lee. The quote perfectly summarized Washington's place in the history of the United States: "First in war, first in peace, and first in the hearts of his countrymen."

What Do You Know!

At the time of his death in 1799, Washington had become one of the largest landowners in the United States, with thousands and thousands of acres of land. About 270 slaves worked on his plantations.

Named in Honor

In 1800, the capital of the United States was moved from Philadelphia to the newly developed city of Washington, D.C., which was named in honor of George Washington. In 1853, Congress created the Washington Territory, which became a state in 1889. It was named in memory of the nation's fiercely loved first president. This is the only state in the United States that is named after an individual American.

The Father of Our Country

Thirty-two counties in various states were later named after George Washington. In 1884, a huge stone column was erected in Washington, D.C., in his memory. This monument, called the Washington Monument, is about 555 feet (169 m) high. Throughout the United States, his memory lives on in the countless streets, parks, and schools named after him. George Washington's legacy is one of the greatest in American history, and he will always be remembered as "The Father of Our Country."

Washington Monument

Washington quarter

GLOSSARY

accessibility being able to access

acquire to get or come by; to buy

alliance an agreement among two or more nations for military or other aid

amendment official additions to a legal document

assemblies bodies of elected representatives that make laws; in the colonies, the form of colonial government

boycott to refuse to buy, often for a political purpose

casualty a soldier or civilian who is injured or killed during a war

chaos confusion, disorder

charter to give rights or privileges to, often by an official government decision

colonies settlements or territories governed by a mother country, often overseas

commend to praise or compliment, often in a proclamation or legislative act

consensus broad agreement;

deploy to send troops or military force out

desertion leaving without permission, often from the military

distilled having been heated and condensed in a process called distillation; the final form of an alcohol

dysentery a digestive disease caused by a bacteria or an amoeba, and causing diarrhea, stomach pain, and bloody stool; can be fatal

economy the exchange of goods, services, and money

equalize to make equal; to ensure equal treatment

ensure to make sure of

eulogy a speech given in memory of a dead person; a speech given at a funeral praising and remembering the deceased

expedition a trip taken for a definite intention; the people making that trip

fertile able to support life; able to grow crops

foreign affairs how different nations relate to each other

formidable intimidating or impressive; difficult to defeat

frontier the edge of the settled world

heir apparent the person who will probably receive a title or an inheritance when the current holder dies; often the oldest son or closest relative

Hessian a hired soldier, or mercenary, from Hesse in modern-day Germany; hired by Britain during the Revolutionary War

honorary rank the military title given in recognition for service; does not offer any particular command or power

House of Burgesses the Virginia legislature, or representative body that makes laws, during the colonial period; made up of two representatives from each Virginia settlement

inaugurate to swear into office

independence the state of being free or uninfluenced by another; often means a self-governing nation

indigenous native; previously existing or living in a place

invoke to call upon; to justify actions under a law or principle

legislative having to do with the legislature, or representative body that makes laws

militia a military unit made up of citizen soldiers, or everyday people with some military experience

national treasury the governmental organization which oversees the nation's money

natural resources a usable good from nature; for example: timber, water, coal

neutral not taking a side; not on one side or the other

patriotism loyalty to one's country or nation

plantation a large estate supported by agriculture; in the colonies often supported by slave labor

precedent a standard that has been set before

prominent important, very visible

provisional for the meantime; a temporary fix

ratify to official approve, often a legal process

repeal to cancel a law

republic a government system in which the citizens elect representatives to make and carry out laws

resistance defiance; actions taken to oppose an authority

resolution a official statement of principle, often adopted by a government or legislature

retreat to turn back or leave, often when losing a battle

settler a person who travels to establish a new home; a person who lives in a settlement

skirmish a fight or clash; often a small clash between enemy soldiers but not large enough to be called a battle

slogan a word or phrase used to inspire action or summarize a larger thought

smallpox a disease caused by a virus and causing fever, headaches, back pain, and lesions on the skin and often death

strategy the science of commanding an army; the use of specific tactics in certain situations

superpower a nation which has significant influence over regional and world events; one of the most powerful nations in the world

surrender to give up; to lay down arms

surveying exactly determining the area and shape of the earth's surface and accurately drawing maps; a field of applied mathematics

surveyor one who takes measurements by surveying and constructs accurate replicas on paper

tuberculosis a lung disease caused by a bacteria and causing the lungs to break down; characterized by coughing up blood and, during the colonial era, death

unanimously with total agreement

unified united; strongly bound; standing together

unprovoked without cause or reason; without provocation

withdraw to draw back or retreat

TIMELINE

1657		George Washington's great-grandfather, John Washington, travels to Virginia
1731		Augustine Washington, John Washington's grandson, marries Mary Ball
1732	*February 22*	George Washington born in Virginia
1743		Augustine Washington dies
1749		George becomes the official surveyor of Culpepper County, Va.
1752		George's half-brother, Lawrence, dies
1753	*October*	George becomes a major in the Virginia militia
1754		French and Indian War begins
1755	*February*	George is sent to serve as assistant and advisor to Gen. Braddock
	July 13	Gen. Braddock mortally wounded in an ambush
	August	George is appointed commander of all Virginia military forces
1758		George resigns as commander of the Virginia forces
1759	*January 6*	George marries Martha Dandridge Custis
1765	*March 27*	Parliament passes the Stamp Act
1770	*March 5*	Boston Massacre
1774		Intolerable Acts are passed
1775	*April 19*	Revolutionary War begins
	June 15	George appointed major general and commander in chief of the colonial forces
1777	*December*	George withdraws his army to Valley Forge, Pa.
1781	*October 19*	British troops surrender at Yorktown, Va.
1787	*May 25*	George presides over the Constitutional Convention
1789	*February 4*	George becomes the first president of the United States
1791	*December 15*	Congress passes the Bill of Rights
1793	*April 22*	George issues the Proclamation of Neutrality
1796	*September 19*	George's *Farewell Address* is published
1797	*March 4*	George finishes his second term as president of the United States John Adams is sworn in as president and Thomas Jefferson as vice president
1799	*December 14*	George dies in his Mount Vernon home

FURTHER READING AND WEBSITES

Books

Allen, Thomas. *George Washington, Spymaster: How the Americans Outspied the British and Won the Revolutionary War.* National Geographic Children's Books, 2007.

Aloian, Molly. *Phillis Wheatley: Poet of the Revolutionary Era.* Crabtree Publishing Company, 2013.

Anderson, Laurie Halse. *Forge (Seeds of Change).* Simon and Schuster, 2010.

Clarke, Gordon. *Significant Battles of the American Revolution.* Crabtree Publishing Company, 2013.

Cocca, Lisa Colozza. *Marquis de Lafayette: Fighting for America's Freedom.* Crabtree Publishing Company, 2013

Edwards, Roberta. *Who Was George Washington?* Grosset and Dunlap, 2009.

Mason, Helen. *Life on the Homefront during the American Revolution.* Crabtree Publishing Company, 2013.

Murray, Stuart. *Eyewitness American Revolution.* Dorling Kindersley Publishing, 2005.

Perritano, John. *The Causes of the American Revolution.* Crabtree Publishing Company, 2013.

Perritano, John. *The Outcome of the American Revolution.* Crabtree Publishing Company, 2013.

Rinaldi, Ann. *Hang a Thousand Trees with Ribbons The Story of Phillis Wheatley.* New York Gulliver Books, 1996

Roberts, Steve. *King George III: England's Struggle to Keep America.* Crabtree Publishing Company, 2013.

Schanzer, Rosalyn. *George vs. George: The American Revolution Seen from Both Sides.* National Geographic Children's Books, 2007.

Woodruff, Elvira. *George Washington's Socks.* Scholastic Paperbacks, 1993.

Websites

"George Washington." *America: The Story of Us.*
www.history.com/shows/america-the-story-of-us/videos/george-washington

"Rediscovering George Washington." *PBS.*
www.pbs.org/georgewashington/

"Facts about George Washington"
www.buzzle.com/articles/facts-about-george-washington.html

"Liberty! The American Revolution." *PBS.*
www.pbs.org/ktca/liberty/

BIBLIOGRAPHY

Books

Chernow, Ron. *Washington: A Life.* Penguin: 2010.

Collier, Christopher and James Lincoln Collier. *Decision in Philadelphia. The Constitutional Convention of 1787.* Ballantine: 2007.

Ellis, Joseph J. *His Excellency: George Washington.* Vintage: 2005.

Ferling, John E. *Almost A Miracle: The American Victory in the War of Independence.* Oxford University Press, 2009.

Griffith, Samuel B. *The War for American Independence: From 1760 to the Surrender at Yorktown in 1781.* University of Illinois Press: 2002.

Lengel, Edward G. *General George Washington: A Military Life.* Random House: 2007.

Lengel, Edward G. (ed). *This Glorious Struggle: George Washington's Revolutionary War Letters.* Smithsonian: 2008.

Randall, Willard Sterne. *George Washington: A Life.* Holt: 1998.

Washington, George. *George Washington: Writings.* Library of America, 1997.

Websites

"George Washington," *Colonial Williamsburg.* **http://www.history.org/almanack/people/bios/biowash2.cfm**

"A Brief Biography of George Washington." *Mount Vernon.* **http://www.mountvernon.org/meet-george-washington/biography-and-influence**

"George Washington." *The White House.* **http://www.whitehouse.gov/about/presidents/georgewashington**

"The Papers of George Washington." *University of Virginia.* **http://gwpapers.virginia.edu/index.html**

Index